CW00661366

PESTLE ANALYSIS

Understand and plan
for your business environment

Written by Thomas del Marmol
In collaboration with Brigitte Feys
Translated by Carly Probert

Business 50MINUTES.com

PESTLE ANALYSIS

KEY INFORMATION

- **Names:** PESTLE analysis, PESTEL analysis, PESTLE framework.
- **Uses:** the PESTLE analysis enables a manager to identify the key macroeconomic factors that may have an influence on the future development of the business.
- **Why is it successful?** The identification of future macroeconomic variables that might be of interest and the construction of different scenarios allow the manager to better anticipate the strategic decisions needed to ensure the proper development and sustainability of the business.
- **Key words:**
  - Competitive advantage: an asset that allows an organisation to stand out positively and get ahead of its competitors in a particular sector.
  - Competitive strategy: methodology implemented with the aim of maximising the success of the business through innovation and greater advantages than those of the competition.
  - Economic situation: the overall position of an entity, determined by all of its political, economic and social elements.
  - Pivot variable: an element of crucial importance that can greatly influence the development of the company.
  - Scenario: the likely theoretical projection for the near or distant future.

INTRODUCTION

The company and its environment

Characterised by an ever-changing environment, our current society differs in many ways from what it was before. Adapting to the changing and competitive environment has now become a necessity for any manager wanting to keep their business afloat and help it to prosper in the coming years. The environment (macroeconomic dimension) has actually proven itself to be a source of both opportunities and threats for any company on the market, regardless of their industry or sector.

Therefore, a confirmed anticipation of the lambda macroeconomic phenomenon will soon provide a direct competitive advantage for the manager, if this allows them to react efficiently before their competitors. On the other hand, if a manager underestimates a momentous event in the market, they will quickly find themselves struggling against competitors whose forecasts are more complete, as they will have to face their competitive and aggressive strategies. For example, companies that did not anticipate the expansion and opportunities offered by the internet in time had a hard time at the turn of the millennium.

As the ability to predict certain future events seems to be the key to the success, good development and even, in some cases, the survival of a company, there are always people who claim, after a change in the environment, that the indicators were inevitably moving in that direction anyway. Yet anticipating these indicators is far from easy, and nobody has a crystal ball for predicting the future.

It is in this context of uncertainty that the PESTLE analysis has appeared, aiming to identify and analyse the macroeconomic variable relevant to an organisation in a specific environment.

Definition of the model

The analysis was given the name PESTLE in reference to the acronym formed by the initials of the six categories of macroeconomic variables included in the model (**P**olitical, **E**conomic, **S**ocio-cultural, **T**echnological, **L**egal and **E**nvironmental). Firstly, the model allows managers to identify the macroeconomic variables to take into consideration for the development of the business (opportunities vs. potential risks), whose likelihood is still relatively uncertain. Then, the model can help the manager to start conceptualising different scenarios based on these uncertain variables to better predict what might happen and make the right decisions now for the future.

WHAT IS THE MACRO-ENVIRONMENT?

The environment of an organisation can be divided into three distinct layers:

- competitors and the market;
- industry (i.e. the corporate sector);
- the macro-environment, the highest-level layer, which consists of broad environmental factors that impact to a greater or lesser extent almost

all organisations. (Johnson et al., 2008).

The layers of an organisation's environment

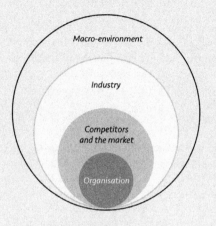

PESTLE Analysis © 50MINUTES.com

THEORY

CONTEXT AND CONCEPT

The origin of the PESTLE analysis remains relatively unclear. However, some authors agree that the first traces of its appearance can be found in the book by Francis J. Aguilar, *Scanning the Business Environment* (1967). At that time, the model was called the PEST analysis, which corresponds to the initial categories of macroeconomic variables: political, economic, socio-cultural and technological.

It was used and perfected during the 1970s and 1980s by several notable authors: Liam Fahey (director of the consultancy organisation Leadership Forum Inc. and professor of management at Boston College), Vadake K. Narayanan (professor of management at Drexel University) and Arnold Brown (consulting project manager) to name but a few. From these different works, various extensions of the initial model appeared under the names of the PEST, SLEPT or STEEPLE analysis. In the end, the additional variables of 'legal' and 'environmental' were retained, resulting in the PESTLE model, which is the most widely accepted today. However, note that some prefer to combine the 'political' and 'legal' aspects under the single term 'political legal', creating the acronym PESTE.

The collection of variables

Since this is a popular and regularly used model, both for completing business plans, production or marketing strategies, and for launching new projects (e.g. when developing a new product on a market that the company has not yet entered), the approach must be specific.

The primary objective of the PESTLE analysis is the identification of unavoidable macroeconomic changes that might have a significant impact on the development of a company (in terms of its products, its brand or even its entire organisation). Therefore, it is not about conducting a comprehensive study of the external environment: the in-depth analysis of macroeconomic variables is only relevant in relation to a specific company, so that it can anticipate the changes that are likely to occur on its scale.

Indeed, of all the macroeconomic events that will occur in the coming years, only some of them will exert a real influence on the evolution of the company. Therefore, it is the manager's responsibility to distinguish between the variables that can directly or indirectly affect the organisation and those that will only have a minor impact on its sustainability. Hence, an executive at the head of an oil company will not react to the recent discoveries on the contributions of shale gas in the same way as an executive of a shipping company, or the owner of a sandwich shop!

Macroeconomic variables are classified into six distinct, though relatively interdependent, categories.

The 6 variables of the PESTLE analysis

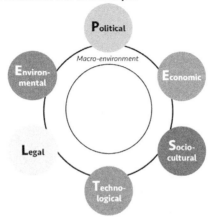

- **Political variables.** The political trends in a country (government pressure, monetary policy, etc.) significantly influence the company that chooses to set itself up there: established public authorities are making more and more decisions that can have a direct impact on daily operations and the prospects of a company's financial (notional interest, etc.) and social (employment assistance, subsidies, etc.) aspects. Other elements, such as conflict, the level of corruption, or the degree of state intervention should also be considered. Furthermore, an entrepreneur who launches a commercial business in a country with perpetual governmental conflict should ensure that they respond to the needs of the indigenous inhabitants, which will be different from those living in a country with stability and peace. Also note that there are bodies such as the European Commission and the World Trade Organization (WTO) that govern international trade policies.

- **Economic variables.** While it is virtually impossible for a company to change the economic situation, it can definitely make preparations in order to better deal with fluctuations. Observing the evolution of a country's GDP, its tax rates and the growth of the inhabitants' purchasing power will prove crucial in possessing all the factors necessary for managerial decision-making. The economic success of a business also involves the observation of key figures relevant to the sector and the analysis of consumer trends. Thus, anticipating a significant decrease in purchasing power allows the company to adapt its overall strategy to minimise losses.

- **Socio-cultural variables.** Knowing the characteristics of a population (demographics, age distribution, etc.) in order to understand its buying behaviour is essential for conquering a market. Moreover, history (roots and traditions) as well as religious and socio-cultural influences (fashion, media, means of communication, etc.) allow the company to refine their analysis of the specific needs of the individuals involved. For example, nationals of Mediterranean countries develop different needs in many ways to those of their counterparts in the Baltic countries due to their culture, the climate in which they live or their religion.

- **Technological variables.** Today, many experts are busy working in every corner of the planet, seeking to revolutionise existing processes. While some of these findings are not likely to influence the target market, others have the potential to completely overturn the norm. The internet revolution came as a surprise to many managers, and those who anticipated its increased use gained a significant competitive advantage. Therefore, it seems natural to investigate the practices in R&D (research and development) and innovation in the chosen field (core business) of the company. Continually reassessing the product, as well as the processes involved in its preparation and acquisition by the customer, is the key to successful technological observation.

- **Legal variables.** Staying informed of regulations (labour laws, trade laws, etc.) in the country where the company is or will be located – as legislation varies from one place to another – is now one of the best ways to protect the company from possible legal attacks and act in the best way possible within legal constraints. For example, regulations concerning the carrying of weapons are not the same in every country, and any astute trader wishing to engage in this sector will quickly adapt their communication and distribution according to the legislation in force in the country concerned. Tax incentives may also lead a well-informed manager to lean towards some countries rather than others.
- **Environmental variables.** The 21st century is a continuation of the 20th, positioning the environment and sustainable development at the heart of debates more than ever. The worrying climate change, constantly increasing pollution, waste sorting that varies from one country to another, etc.: nowadays these aspects interest and

preoccupy more and more people and those who lead them. This concern sometimes has a direct impact on the commercial world. The controlling of energy use or pollution levels are two examples of the many measures taken by regional, national and/or international authorities. These can influence the course of an organisation's operations. Meanwhile, new markets are created: for example, in the case of organic products.

The table below shows a summary of the major macroeconomic variables for each identified category. This non-exhaustive list should be completed according to the corporate sector and specific countries of each company.

Examples of PESTLE macroeconomic variables

Political
Conflict, political instability, war, corruption, the level of state intervention, etc.

Economic
Business cycle, growth rate, interest rate, country GDP, inflation, taxation, unemployment, purchasing power, etc.

Socio-cultural
Demographic, history, religion, distribution of income, age distribution, lifestyle (trends), education, health, emigration,

Technological
Innovations, investments in R&D, technical cycle, new scientific discoveries and patents, energy costs, etc.

Legal
Country legislation, jurisdiction, tax, social security, legal security, regulations, etc.

Environmental
Environmental standards, renewable energy, climate change, awareness, security training, recycling incentives, transport impact, etc.

PESTLE Analysis © 50MINUTES.com

Identifying pivot variables

The main difficulty of the exercise lies in identifying the relevant variables in relation to a specific company. The risk, if the sorting is not done well, is ending up with so much information that one cannot pay due attention to each of them and will therefore miss opportunities or imminent threats. Therefore, it is essential to identify the pivot variables in order to better understand the crucial upcoming events for the company.

The pivot variables are 'the factors that could significantly affect the structure of an industry or a market' (Johnson et al, 2008: 64). These variables are consequently different according to the type of industry and market – although some argue that all companies face the same threats, as the globalisation of markets continues to grow and bodies governing international trade are constantly being created. Moreover, they vary over time, which leads to a perpetual questioning of the data used. Whether on the level of consumer tastes or the economic situation, working in a volatile environment forces the manager to regularly consult or ask for market research or to go out 'into the field' to verify the relevance of these variables.

Constructing scenarios

Once the data is collected, identified and classified, based on the pivot variables, according to their probability and potential impact, the manager will have to construct scenarios. They represent possible alternatives for the future of the company. For example, one of the pivot variables of the real estate sector is directly linked to mortgage rates enabling individuals to make their investments. In this case, the head of a construction company will imagine different scenarios: one in which the rate increases slightly, a second in which it strongly decreases, a third in which it stagnates, etc.

ADVANTAGES

Although the PESTLE analysis does not claim to predict what the future holds, it does however prove useful for initiating proactive and constructive discussions about the future of the company. The appropriate use of this tool makes it possible to detect potential opportunities and threats for the company, which can quickly turn into a significant competitive advantage. The PESTLE model favours a comprehensive view, the opportunity to take a step back and a certain amount of flexibility.

The use of scenarios is particularly useful when there are a low number of pivot variables with a high degree of uncertainty. These can lead to two radically different futures for the company and it is up to the manager to correctly identify the answers to each of them and, above all, their potential contribution to the company's performance. Depending on the different scenarios described, it is possible to anticipate the ideal reactions in the case of either of them materialising. It also makes sense to quantify the probability of each scenario occurring, in order to prepare in advance the elements necessary for the success of the company in the most probable scenario.

Once the different scenarios have been identified, it is up to the manager and his advisers to thoroughly analyse each of them, to assess the likelihood of their materialisation and the direct impact this would have on the company.

PRACTICAL APPLICATION

ADVICE AND TOP TIPS

Information sorting and development

Collecting macroeconomic data sometimes involves the inclusion of information that is not always completely reliable. It is therefore strongly advised that the manager immediately tests its ground truth in order to check that it is correct. In this case, it is also essential to constantly compare the information gathered with the new market data.

It appears, with regards to the classification suggested above, that many variables are interdependent. Indeed, the introduction of a pollution tax concerns both the legal and environmental aspects. Similarly, the appearance of new technology can affect certain economic and socio-cultural aspects of a country. Thus, even if the suggested classification is useful for the manager – who is required to sort between the variables – it need not be applied systematically in every detail. As a matter of fact, the importance of classifying variables into one category or another is relative: for example, spending hours deciding whether the fiscal policy of a country is related more to the political, economic or legal categories is of no major interest. As it is primarily a structured method of listing the various macro-economic influences on the company, the real challenge lies in identifying the relevance of this data and its potential impact on the organisation. To facilitate the sorting of information, it can also be useful to make comparisons with past events that have had an impact on the sector.

The construction of scenarios provides a comprehensive view of possible future situations, but should not be carried out too specifically in any case: the PESTLE analysis does not attempt to dictate specific guidelines, but rather initiate discussions about the possible strategic decisions to take in case a situation described in one of the scenarios materialises. It is generally advisable to choose an even number of scenarios (two or four) in order to avoid the temptation of favouring the intermediate scenario.

Applications

There are many times and situations where a PESTLE analysis is appropriate:

- **The launch of a new business.** Creating a business plan, which is necessary for convincing shareholders to invest in the company, requires the use of strategic tools to demonstrate a thorough analysis of the market and its consumer appeal. In this context, the PESTLE analysis may prove to investors that the macroeconomic environment is favourable to the development of a company on the market, or, if this is not the case, at least draw their attention to the fact that the company is aware of the risk variables and there is a way to compensate for them.
- **The development of new products or the launch of new projects.** Similarly, the PESTLE analysis allows the manager to assess if the environment is ready to welcome a new product onto the market. The decision to undertake a new project may also be the subject of a

detailed analysis.

- **Reassessing the organisation of the company.** The choices made during the creation of the company may rapidly become obsolete in the face of the constant evolution of most markets. Indeed, the tastes of the population can quickly change, economic conditions fluctuate, new technologies appear, etc. The company's strategy should be continuously reassessed, by making regular updates to the PESTLE analysis and other diagnostic tools, to include recent events.

- **The decision-making process of the marketing strategy.** Being knowledgeable about the macroeconomic variables of a sector, particularly on a socio-cultural level, can be crucial for communicating properly with its audience. What are the region's cultural norms? What is the history of the country? These questions will help to avoid costly mistakes in time and money for the company wanting to see their product adopted by a section of the population.

Extrapolation

The collected variables will be interpreted in different ways depending on the experience and background of the people analysing them. An economist will not perceive the implications of a change in government in the same way as a lawyer or sociologist.

Since the interaction of experts allows for optimal anticipation of the implications of a newly identified variable, it becomes essential to work with the right people.

Analysing the sector

The preparatory work carried out using the PESTLE analysis helps the manager to make the relevant decisions in the field, those that will ensure the sustainability of the company. They will have a direct and indirect impact on the processes and the work of all members of the organisation.

Therefore, the decisions made using the framework of the PESTLE analysis should be shared with the entire organisation, in order to bring the team together around a common vision that is understood and taken on board by all. The support of the whole organisation is perhaps one of the major keys to success regarding decisions arising from the PESTLE analysis. The implementation of decisions made regarding daily business life will be facilitated.

CASE STUDY

Belgian Post Group (bpost)

In 1790, the municipal post office appeared in Belgium. Its activities continuously developed until it became the public limited company bpost that we know today. Although the reform in 1963 requiring each home to have a mailbox provided a real boost for the development of regular post, the company has been facing new challenges since the early 2000s. The emergence of new means of communication and the increasingly popular use of the internet somewhat changed the situation in a sector where paper once dominated. Moreover, whereas bpost once monopolised the market for post, competition opened up in 2011, once again shaking up the operational modes that bpost was accustomed to.

It was in this disrupted context that the company decided to launch a new service in 2013: the *Shop and Deliver* or 'bpost by appointment', which aims to deliver shopping to customers' homes according to orders placed beforehand on their website. To do so, the goal of the company is to form partnerships with traders already established on the market in order to satisfy the maximum number of people. Bpost thus builds on its existing long-term relationship of trust with its stakeholders: on the one hand, the company offers a medium to sellers, much like an e-commerce platform, allowing them to reach people doing their shopping online and, on the other hand, bpost mail customers benefit from a home delivery service of their shopping on weekdays between 5pm and 9pm. They can select their products on the internet and choose a delivery location and a time slot for the single price of €9.95 per parcel.

The completed PESTLE analysis

As discussed above, when deciding to launch a new project, it may be wise to use the PESTLE analysis in order to fully understand the ins and outs of future macroeconomic variables. In this case, the relevant variables selected for this analysis refer to the launch of the *Shop and Deliver* project that bpost wishes to implement.

Relevant macroeconomic variables for bpost

Political

- Suppression of aid linked to general services of interest
- Restructuring of public companies
- Belgian governmental stability?

Economic

- Economic crisis and the decrease of domestic mail
- Stagnation of economic growth
- Requirements of stock exchange listings (2013)

Socio-cultural

- Predominance of social partners (unions) in the sector
- Growing use of new technology (smartphones, tablets, etc.)
- Generation gap between the 'baby boomers' and Generation Y
- Ageing population
- Evolution of morals regarding employment

Technological

- Growth of e-commerce
- Automation and robotization
- Development of new sorting centers

Legal

- Tougher anti-monopoly laws
- Opening of the mail market to competition (1st January 2011)
- Consecutive legal obligations for NYSE-Euronext listings
- Fixed stamp tariffs

Environmental

- The need to be responsible in society
- Poor image for supporting paper as a means of communication
- Classification attributed by the International Environmental Post Corporation

PESTLE Analysis © 50MINUTES.com

Constructing scenarios

Once the unknown variables have been identified, the manager will construct different scenarios to anticipate the likely evolution of these variables and their impact on the company. Given the high number of variables collected for this case study, we will focus on constructing four scenarios for the socio-cultural variables.

The project's success depends on both the acceptance of the service by the general public and the expansion of sales via e-commerce. The fulfilment of these two conditions is based on a number of incalculable aspects, which is why it is essential to construct different scenarios. The diagram below shows the different scenarios of evolution for the company based on the materialisation of the variables.

Likely future scenarios for the bpost company

	Expansion of e-commerce sales	Reduction of e-commerce sales
Public acceptance	Complete success	Limited success
Public rejection	Great frustration	Complete failure

PESTLE Analysis © 50MINUTES.com

Henceforth, the company can envisage all eventualities: the manager must then be prepared to respond in the best way possible to each scenario and provide tailored solutions in case one should occur.

Conclusion

- In conclusion, although bpost remains a company mostly owned by the Belgian State, over the years it has gained increasing independence so that it can no longer survive on public aid or on its assets, which fully encourages it to become highly competitive.
- Its core business suffers from a poor image as well as less activity due to many adverse factors. It has every interest in using technological prowess and its profitability (17.96% normalised EBIT margin in 2013) to operate a series of strategic diversifications, including *Shop and Deliver,* to prepare for the lifestyle changes of consumers who are using e-commerce more and more to make their purchases.
- The company's *Shop and Deliver* activity will provide additional income, enabling it to diversify its sources of profit. The project proposal has been approved by management: currently in the development stage, it will be suitably launched in the coming months. Only time will tell whether this project results in success or dismal failure.
- Although the use of the PESTLE analysis is indeed relevant in this case, it remains insufficient. In fact, this analysis must be complemented by an extensive investigation into the strengths and weaknesses of the company to identify its main assets in its pursuit of integration into its environment and profitability: threats and opportunities (SWOT analysis) as well as the opening of the market to competition (Porter's five (+1) forces analysis) should be duly considered in order to avoid overlooking any aspects

and to get the best possible forecasts.

LIMITATIONS AND EXTENSIONS

LIMITATIONS AND CRITICISMS

Although the model is very popular among business managers, the PESTLE analysis, like any other strategic model, nevertheless has its share of limitations.

- **Relative global vision.** One of the main limitations is actually the result of one of the model's most popular benefits: wishing to cover a broad spectrum of macroeconomic variables, the manager can quickly find themselves overwhelmed by the amount of information they are inevitably faced with. As a matter of fact, there is a huge difference between stressing the importance of sorting the relevant macroeconomic variables and doing this in practice. At a certain point, all of the variables seem important and the number of scenarios to construct is so high that Steve Jobs himself would struggle to draw relevant conclusions! Being competent is not always enough to identify pivot variables. Sometimes it is necessary to have good intuition and to question it: for example, surrounding yourself with a multidisciplinary team capable of developing collective intelligence and counting on a good deal of luck. Nevertheless, luck can be influenced by working rigorously and analysing as broadly as possible.
- **Unreliable scenarios.** Situations are often different in practice as opposed to in theory, and what is predicted does not always coincide with reality. From this angle, the tool seems useful, but does not possess any concrete reliability.

- **Lack of objectivity.** It has been observed that many managers opt to implement three separate scenarios for a pivot variable: an optimistic scenario, a pessimistic scenario and a middle scenario. Although this tactic gives the manager the impression that he is being as objective as possible when developing a strategy, in reality, this often forces him to ignore the other two scenarios in favour of the middle scenario. And what is the use in constructing several scenarios if we are ultimately only concerned with one of them?
- **Impact that is impossible to quantify.** Finally, be aware that while it is possible to determine the major macroeconomic changes that could affect the market using this model, the specific impact of these variables on the sector remains difficult to judge and even more difficult to quantify.

RELATED MODELS AND EXTENSIONS

As the PESTLE analysis only concerns one of the three levels of the organisation's environment, an analysis based solely on its variables cannot be considered relevant for developing a strategy for the company.

Although it seems interesting at first (to identify major trends in the macro-environment), the PESTLE diagnostic should be complemented by other tools that study the close environment of the organisation, i.e. its macro-environment: industry, direct competitors, and so on. Later on, Porter's five (+1) forces analysis and the SWOT analysis complete the reflection on the company's strategy.

Porter five (+1) forces analysis

Developed by the American professor Michael Porter in 1979, the five (+1) forces analysis allows us to observe an industry's attractiveness and identify its competitive behaviours. The model is based on the concept of competitive advantage. Therefore, it is up to the manager to observe the main competitive forces in the industry to understand and better assess the power of each of the current and potential competitors.

WHAT IS COMPETITIVE ADVANTAGE?

The concept of competitive advantage is based on "all the characteristics or attributes held by a product or brand that give it a certain superiority over its immediate competitors. These characteristics or attributes may be varied in nature and relate to the product itself [...], the necessary or added services that accompany the basic service, or the conditions for production, distribution or sales of the product or company" (Lambin and de Moerloose, 2008: 250).

These forces represent:

- the bargaining power of suppliers
- the bargaining power of customers
- the threat of new entrants
- substitute products
- cross-industry competition

- the role of the state (included later).

Porter Five (+1) Forces Analysis

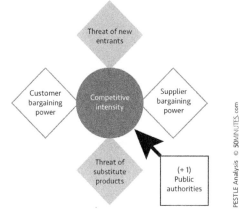

The task of evaluating the relevant forces lies with the manager: the goal is to determine the current and future attractiveness of the sector, i.e. the development prospects and the performance of their business. Generally, Porter's five (+1) forces analysis concludes by identifying the key success factors that allow for optimal development of the company.

SWOT Analysis

Developed in the 1960s by several professors from the Harvard Business School, the SWOT analysis aims to draw the main conclusions from factors of interest related to the company's characteristics and environment. The name of the model is the result of the acronym formed by the words 'Strengths', 'Weaknesses', 'Opportunities' and 'Threats'. Thus, it is the responsibility of the decision-maker to identify the main strengths and weaknesses of the business and to be aware of the opportunities and threats facing the sector.

The interest in the SWOT analysis lies more in its conclusions than in the listing of the characteristics of the business and the sector. For the manager, the conclusions will be any points of interest and points for reflection that will allow for the development of a strategy tailored to the company, with regards to both its internal and external environment.

CONVERGING THE MODELS

A seasoned manager will quickly understand the benefits of the complementary use of these models. While individually they may still be useful, it is actually through the intersection and overlapping of information between them that the main rational strategic decisions can be formulated.

The analysis of the environment follows several stages during which the implementation of certain models will influence the construction of later models. Although collecting information can be tedious, analysing the environment is essential for any company wishing to maintain a sustainable competitive advantage.

Convergence of the models

	STRENGTHS	WEAKNESSES	OPPORTUNITIES	THREATS
Political				
Economic				
Socio-cultural				
Technological				
Legal				
Environmental				

PESTLE Analysis © 50MINUTES.com

SUMMARY

- The first traces of the PESTLE analysis appeared in 1967 in the book *Scanning the Business Environment* by Professor Francis J. Aguilar, under the name PEST analysis. Studied and developed by many authors, it later became the PESTLE model as we know it today.
- The main objectives of the PESTLE analysis are the classification of macroeconomic variables into six categories – **P**olitical, **E**conomic, **S**ocio-cultural, **T**echnological, **L**egal and **E**nvironmental – and taking a step back, which is necessary for anticipating and ensuring the future of a specific company.
  - Observing this data allows you to understand in which environment the business is evolving, or will be evolving in the future. This global and macroeconomic view is valid for all companies.
  - The main difficulty of the model lies in sorting the relevant variables according to the business in question. Their collection leads to the identification of pivot variables that are considered to have a crucial influence on the healthy development of the company, but whose likelihood is still uncertain.
  - Whether used just before launching a new company, for launching a new product or project, reorganising a company or when faced with imminent changes in the environment, the PESTLE analysis provides significant information about the inherent pivot variables of a given situation. Thus, using its observations, the executive will construct a number of scenarios (preferably

an even number) based on the information gathered. The goal is to better anticipate future situations that the company is likely to encounter and to provide solutions to ensure the sustainability and future of the company.

- The PESTLE analysis enables you to initiate a proactive discussion on the future of the company, based on the macroeconomic variables previously collected.
- Using it alone is interesting but insufficient. Porter's five (+1) forces analysis and the SWOT analysis can prove to be a useful aid in the analysis of the business environment (microenvironment).
- The case of the company bpost demonstrates the importance of analysing whether the environment is favorable for the launch of a new project when the company is faced with a changing environment.
- Finally, it is important to remember that the PESTLE analysis is a valuable tool, although it cannot predict with certainty what the future holds. However, it does allow companies to identify the major trends in order to better prepare and defend their competitive advantage.

We want to hear from you!
Leave a comment on your online library
and share your favourite books on social media!

FURTHER READING

BIBLIOGRAPHY

- AWT. (2013) *L'e-commerce 2013 en Wallonie.* [Online]. [Accessed 11 May 2015]. Available from Internet Archive: <https://web.archive.org/web/20131202084750/http://www.awt.be/web/dem/index.aspx?page=dem,fr,b13,ent,050>
- Bpost. (2013) *Bpost annual report 2012.* Brussels: Bpost.
- Curau, L. (2012) Avantages concurrentiels : les cinq forces de Porter. *Cafedelabourse.com.* [Online]. [Accessed 11 May 2015]. Available from: <https://www.cafedelabourse.com/dossiers/article/avantages-concurrentiels-les-5-forces-de-porter#>
- Dcosta, A. (2011) PESTLE Analysis History and Application. *Bright Hub Project Management.* [Online]. [Accessed 11 May 2015]. Available from: <http://www.brighthubpm.com/project-planning/100279-pestle-analysis-history-and-application/>
- Duguay, B. (2014) La capacité stratégique. *UQAM.*
- Johnson, G., Scholes, K., Whittington, R. and Fréry, F. (2008) *Stratégique.* [8th edition]. Paris: Pearson Education.
- Kashi, K. and Dočkalíková, I. (2014) MCDM Methods in Practice: Determining Importance of PESTEL Analysis Criteria. *International Days of Statistics and Economics.* [Online]. [Accessed 11 May 2015]. Available from: <http://msed.vse.cz/msed_2014/article/362-Dockalikova-Iveta-paper.pdf>
- Lambin, J.-J. and de Moerloose, C. (2008) *Marketing*

stratégique et opérationnel. Du marketing à l'orientation de marché. [7th edition]. Paris: Dunod.

- Lopez, F. (2011) L'analyse PESTEL. *Actinnovation.* [Online]. [Accessed 11 May 2015]. Available from: <http://www.actinnovation.com/innobox/outils-innovation/analyse-pestel>
- Nadkarni, S. and Narayanan, V. K. (2007) Strategic Schemas, Strategic Flexibility, and Firm Performance: the Moderating Role of Industry Clockspeed. Strategic Management Journal. 28(3), pp. 243-270.
- PESTLEAnalysis. (2014) *What is Pestle Analysis?* [Online]. [Accessed 11 May 2015]. Available from: <http://pestleanalysis.com/>
- Porter, M. E. (2008) The Five Competitive Forces That Shape Strategy. Harvard Business Review. 86(1), pp. 25-40.
- Post&Parcel. (2012) *Bpost Extends Same-Day Home Delivery Trials.* [Online]. [Accessed 11 May 2015]. Available from: <http://postandparcel.info/52078/news/companies/bpost-extends-same-day-home-delivery-trials/>
- Srivastava, R. K., Fahey, L. and Christensen, H. K. (2014) The resource-Based View and Marketing: The Role of Market-Based Assets in Gaining Competitive Advantage. Journal of Management. 27(6), pp. 777-802.

ADDITIONAL SOURCES

- Aguilar, F. J. (1967) *Scanning the Business Environment.* New York: Macmillan.
- *bpost* website.

http://www.bpost.be/site/fr/postgroup/index.html
- *Happycapital* website.
  http://www.happy-capital.com/
- Silva, N. (2012) SWOT Analysis vs PEST Analysis and When to Use Them. *Creately.* [Online]. [Accessed 11 May 2015]. Available from: <http://creately.com/blog/diagrams/swot-analysis-vs-pest-analysis/>
- Walsh, P. R. (2005) Dealing With The Uncertainties of Environmental Change by Adding Scenario Planning to The Strategy Reformulation Equation. *Management Decision.* 43(1), pp. 113-122.
- Yüksel, I. (2012) Developing a Multi-Criteria Decision Making Model for PESTEL Analysis. *International Journal of Business and Management.* 7(24).

www.50minutes.com

Ebook EAN: 9782806268372

Paperback EAN: 9782806270672

Legal Deposit: D/2015/12603/444

Cover: © Primento

Digital conception by Primento, the digital partner of
publishers.

Printed in Great Britain
by Amazon

64593292R00031